Laughapalooza Joke Book

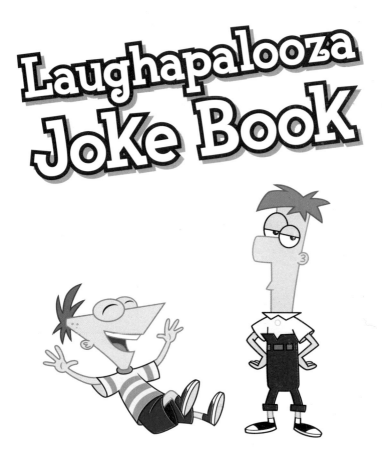

Written by Kitty Richards

Based on the series created by Dan Povenmire & Jeff "Swampy" Marsh

DISNEY XD

Bath · New York · Singapore · Hong Kong · Cologne · Delhi
Melbourne · Amsterdam · Johannesburg · Auckland · Shenzhen

This edition published by Parragon in 2011

Parragon
Queen Street House
4 Queen Street
Bath BA1 1HE, UK

ISBN 978-1-4075-8486-7

Printed in Malaysia

INTRODUCTION

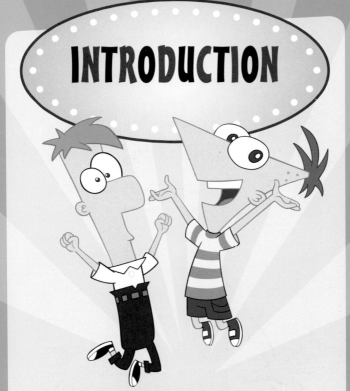

I know what we're gonna do today! We're gonna read this book of jokes. Of course, Candace will try to bust us. She is *always* trying to bust us. *"Mu-um!"* she'll say. "They're up to something!"

But before their mum sees anything, all the evidence will be gone. I don't know exactly what will happen, but I know *something* will. Phineas and Ferb will be part of it, and so will some evil plan by Dr Doofenshmirtz. But luckily, as usual, it's Perry the Platypus (otherwise known as Agent P) to the rescue! It will all be crazy, but in some weird way it will all make sense, too. Meanwhile, you and I have a bunch of jokes to read. So let's turn the page and get started!

But hey . . . where's Perry?

WHAT DID YOU DO DURING *YOUR SUMMER* HOLIDAY?

Did you discover a mummy hidden in the basement of a cinema? Build the world's largest roller coaster? Help your friend build a portal to Mars?

Didn't think so! Well, you know who did? Phineas and Ferb, that's who! These two stepbrothers certainly know how to keep themselves amused. (Even if it does drive their sister, Candace, crazy!)

And when they're not blasting off into outer space or surfing tidal waves in their backyard, there's one thing Phineas and Ferb *really* like to do – share a good joke. And this book is filled with them! So sit back, relax and enjoy the laughs!

Phineas Flynn:

Supercreative, he comes up with all the crazy ideas.

Ferb Fletcher:
Supersmart, he makes all of Phineas's insane
plans a reality. He doesn't talk much.

Candace Flynn:

She is always trying to get her brothers into trouble.
And she has a huge crush on Jeremy Johnson.

Perry the Platypus
(aka Agent P):

The Flynn/Fletcher family pet.
He is also Agent P, and is called on repeatedly to save
the world from the dangerous Dr Doofenshmirtz.

Dr Heinz Doofenshmirtz:

An evil doctor bent on
dominating the Tri-State Area, but his plans usually
get foiled by Agent P.

Major Monogram:

The superior officer of the top secret organization that Perry the Platypus belongs to.

Isabella Garcia-Shapiro:
Friend and leader of the Fireside Girls, she has a huge crush on Phineas. But he has no idea!

Baljeet Rai:

Phineas and Ferb's supersmart friend.

Buford Van Stomm:
The big bad bully.
Watch out!

Django Brown:

Phineas and Ferb's
hippie friend.

The Fireside Girls:

This troop is always in the know and can always be counted on to accompany Phineas and Ferb on their adventures.

Jeremy Johnson:
Candace's supercute crush.

Suzy Johnson:

Jeremy's little sister. But don't be fooled by her adorable appearance. This toddler is trouble. Even Buford is scared of her!

What is Ferb's favourite month of the year?
Ferb-uary, of course!

Phineas: **Knock-knock.**

Candace: **Who's there?**

Phineas: **Yodelay-hee.**

Candace: **Yodelay-hee who?**

Phineas: **I didn't know you could yodel, Candace!**

Candace: **Knock-knock.**

Phineas: **Who's there?**

Candace: **Shirley.**

Phineas: **Shirley who?**

Candace: **Shirley you're not trying to build the world's largest roller coaster in our backyard!**

Isabella: **Knock-knock.**

Phineas: **Who's there?**

Isabella: **Mike.**

Phineas: **Mike who?**

Isabella: **Mike stomach hurts — that roller coaster was one crazy ride!**

Baljeet: **Knock-knock.**

Django: **Who's there?**

Baljeet: **Disguise.**

Django: **Disguise who?**

Baljeet: **Disguise crazy — he
built a haunted house
in his backyard!**

Jeremy: Hey Candace, why did the chocolate-chip cookie go to the doctor?

Candace: I don't know, Jeremy. Why?

Jeremy: He was feeling crummy!

Phineas, Ferb and Candace have a pet platypus named

PERRY

To Phineas and Ferb, Perry is just your ordinary platypus. But little do they know that he also has a secret identity as Agent P – with underground headquarters and tons of supercool spy gear!

His mission? To save the world (or at least the Tri-State Area) from the evil Dr Doofenshmirtz!

What did Agent P say when Dr Doofenshmirtz built a gigantic robot named Norm?

Nothing! Platypuses can't talk!

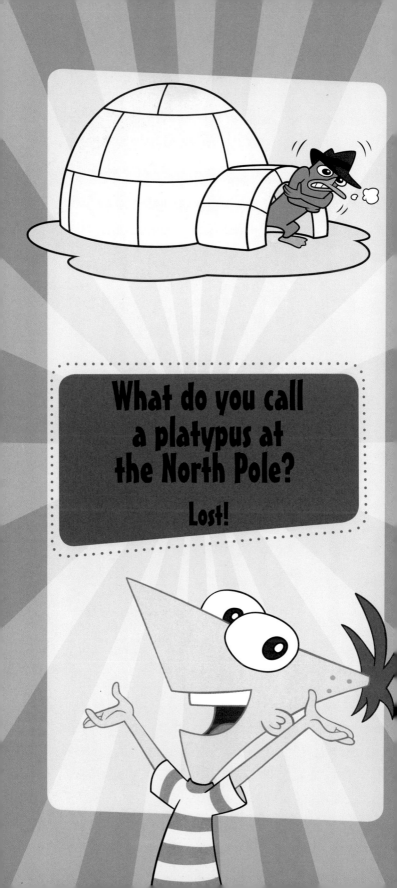

What's the first thing that happens when a platypus falls into a lake?

It gets wet!

What kinds of platypuses can jump higher than a house?

All kinds, houses can't jump!

When can twenty platypuses
be under an umbrella and
not get wet?

When it's sunny out!

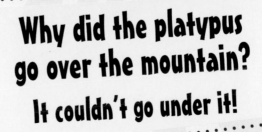

Why did the platypus go over the mountain?

It couldn't go under it!

Perry's archnemesis is

Dr Doofenshmirtz —

the most clueless evil scientist the Tri-State Area has ever seen. Just take a look at a few of his ridiculous plans. He attempted to dig a tunnel to China and set up a toll booth. (He just happened to forget about the Earth's molten centre.) He tried to melt all the chocolate in the Tri-State Area. He tried to destroy all people dressed as sandwiches. You get the picture. And each and every time he is foiled by Agent P. But Dr Doofenshmirtz never gives up. You have to respect him for that, don't you? (Okay, maybe not.)

Doofenshmirtz: Knock knock.

Perry: (makes platypus noise)

Doofenshmirtz: Oh, I forgot that you... well, don't really talk, do you? So if I said, "Orange," then you would say...

Perry: (makes platypus noise)

Doofenshmirtz: Right, right. So I would imagine you said, "Orange who?" and then I would say, "Orange you glad you're not evil like me?"

Perry: (makes platypus noise)

Doofenshmirtz: Yes, yes, I see your point. It's not really what the kids call "funny," is it? Curse you, Perry the Platypus!

What time is it when Dr Doofenshmirtz submerges your home so he'll have lakefront property?

Time to get a new house!

Dr Doofenshmirtz's

outrageous plans make Phineas and Ferb's ideas seem positively normal! Remember the time Phineas and Ferb built an animal translator so they could understand what Perry was saying? They ended up with a backyard full of complaining animals who were finally able to say what was on their minds!

What's black and white and red all over?

An embarrassed zebra!

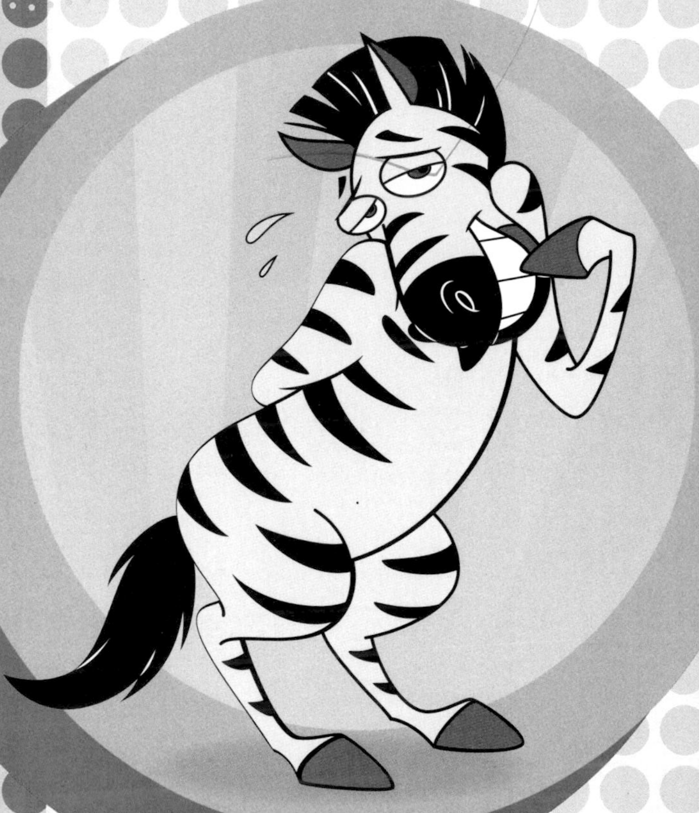

Why don't any of the animals in the jungle ever want to play cards?

There are too many cheetahs!

Why are elephants
so wrinkled?

Have you ever tried to iron one?

How do porcupines play leapfrog?

Very carefully!

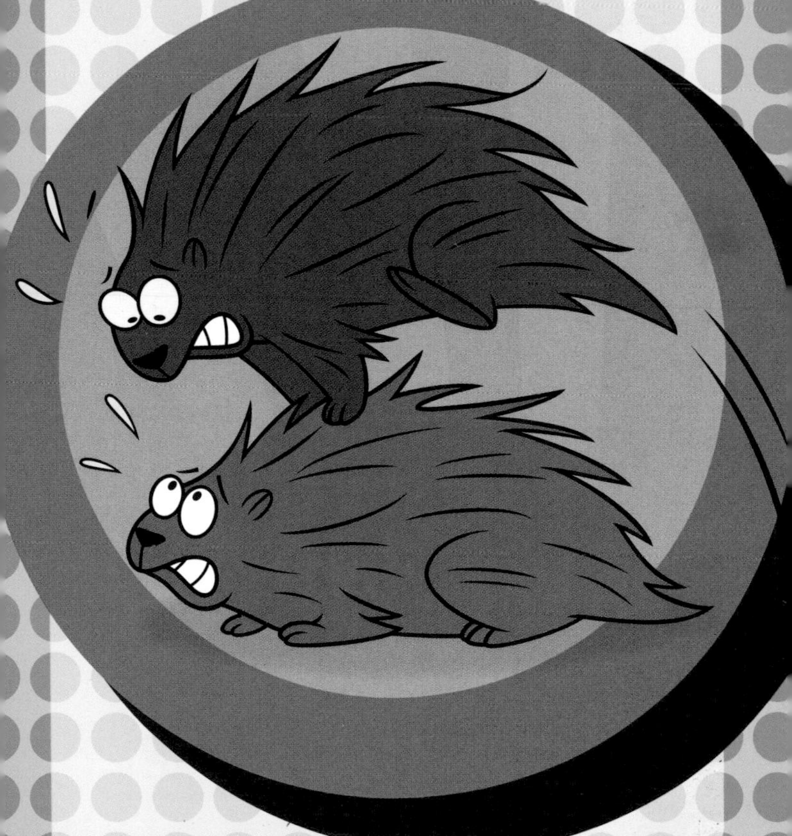

What's smarter than a talking dog?

A spelling bee!

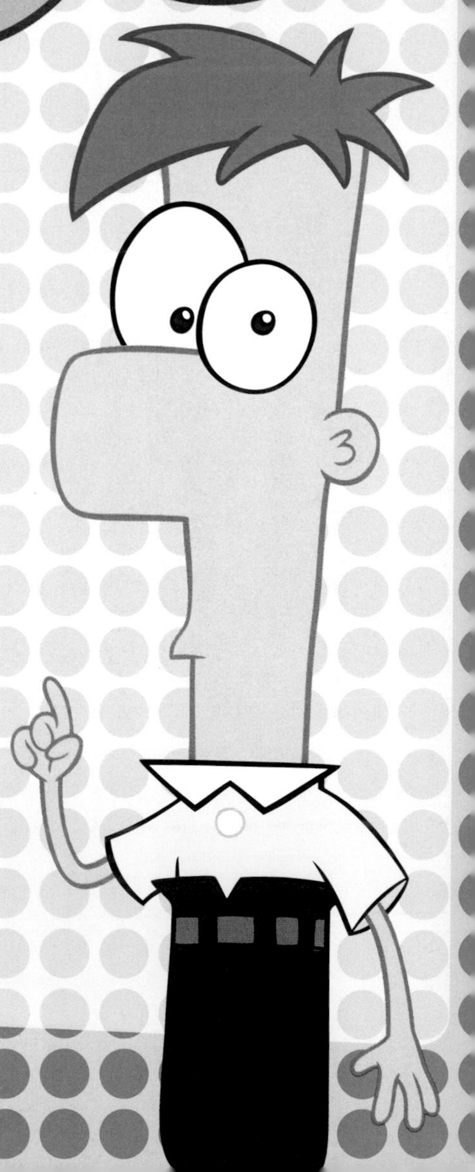

What is a puppy's
favourite swimming
stroke?

The doggy paddle!

What's a bee's favourite sweet?
Bumble gum!

Remember the time

Phineas and Ferb built a humongous haunted house to scare Isabella and cure her hiccups? There were ghosts, vampires and even an awesome *Ferb*-enstein! It was spook-*tacularly* scary!

Why don't vampires have any friends?

Because they are all pains in the neck!

What do you call a skeleton who won't get out of bed?

Lazybones!

Where does a werewolf sit?
Anywhere it wants to!

What kind of dog does Dracula have?

A bloodhound!

What do you say when you meet a two-headed monster?

Hello, hello!

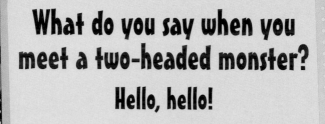

What is a vampire's favourite street to live on?

A dead-end!

How did the skeleton know there was going to be a rainstorm?

He could feel it in his bones!

Or, how about the time

Phineas and Ferb discovered a mummy in the basement of the cinema? (Never mind that it was just Candace wrapped in toilet paper. It turned out to be just as scary!)

Phineas: **Knock-knock.**

Dad: **Who's there?**

Phineas: **Howl.**

Dad: **Howl who?**

Phineas: **Howl we find the missing mummy?**

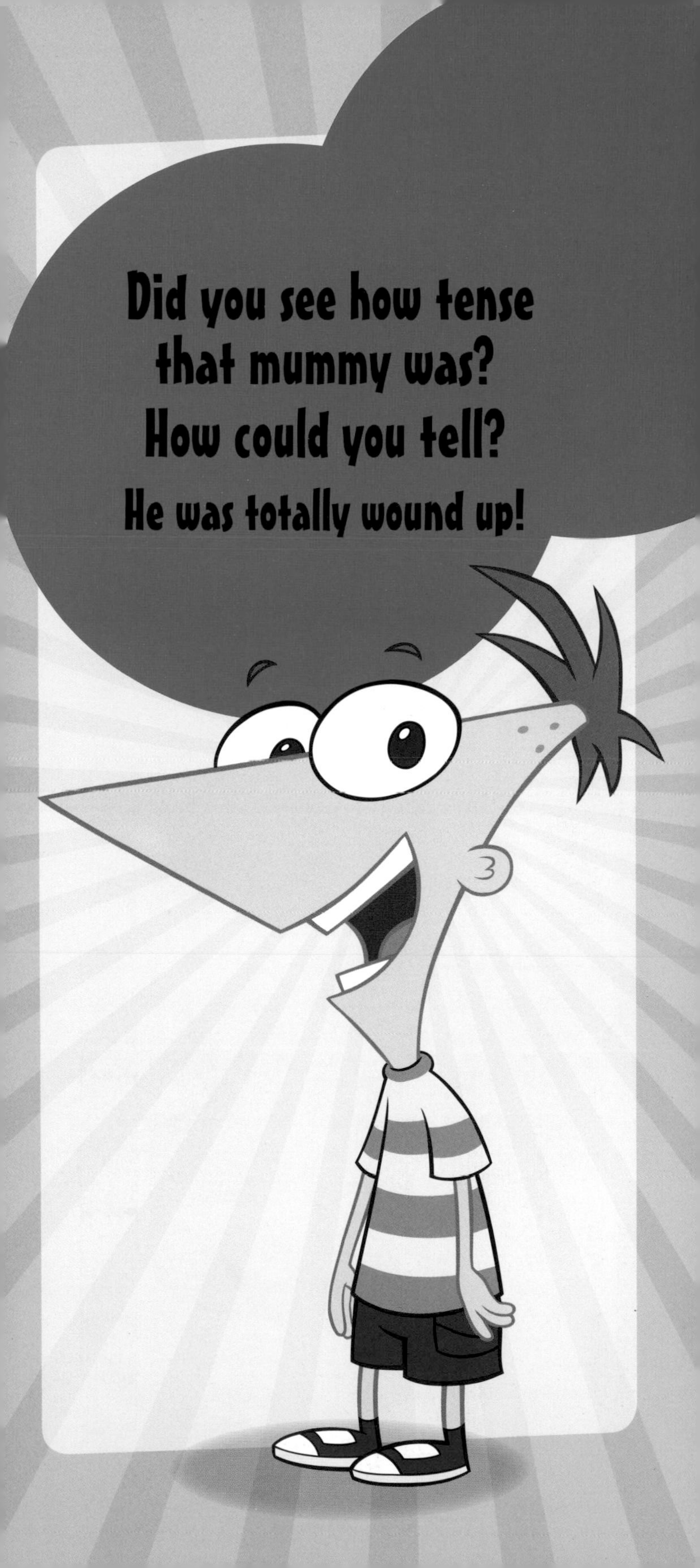
Did you see how tense that mummy was?
How could you tell?
He was totally wound up!

What is a mummy's favourite kind of music?

Wrap music!

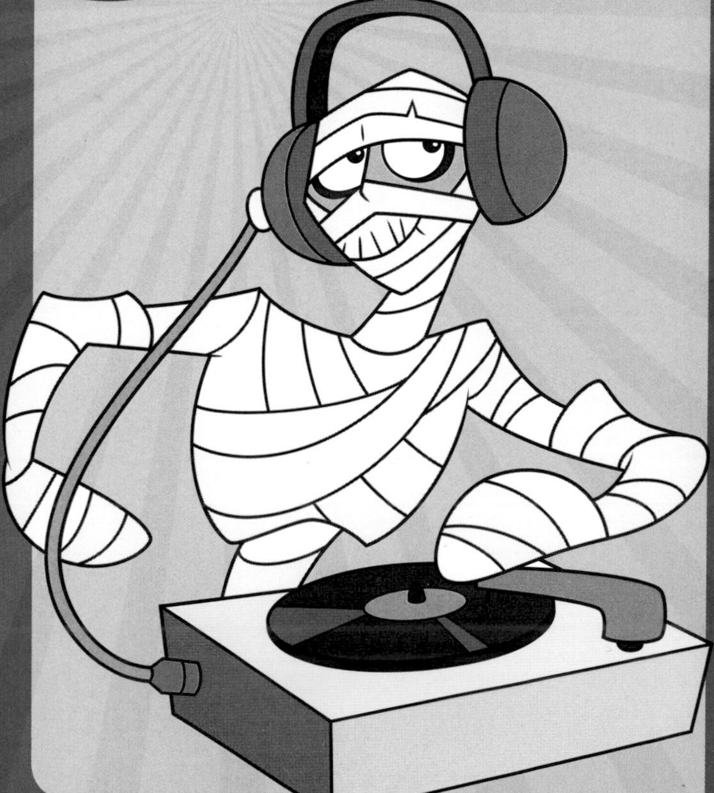

What did the mummy say when it got angry with the skeleton?

I have a bone to pick with you!

Why are mummies good at keeping secrets?

They keep things under wraps!

One day, Phineas and Ferb

decided to build a rocket ship so they could check out a star that their dad had named for them. The best part of space travel, according to Phineas? "The g-forces and eating dinner out of a tube!"

What's the most dangerous thing in outer space?

A shooting star!

What do you call crazy bugs on the moon?

Lunar-tics!

What are planets' favourite kinds of books to read?

Comet books!

Why didn't the moon
finish his dinner?
He was full!

How cool was it when

Phineas, Ferb and Candace travelled back to the time of the dinosaurs? Their time machine was destroyed, and then Candace was chased by an angry T-rex! Luckily, Isabella and the Fireside Girls were able to get them all home safe and sound!

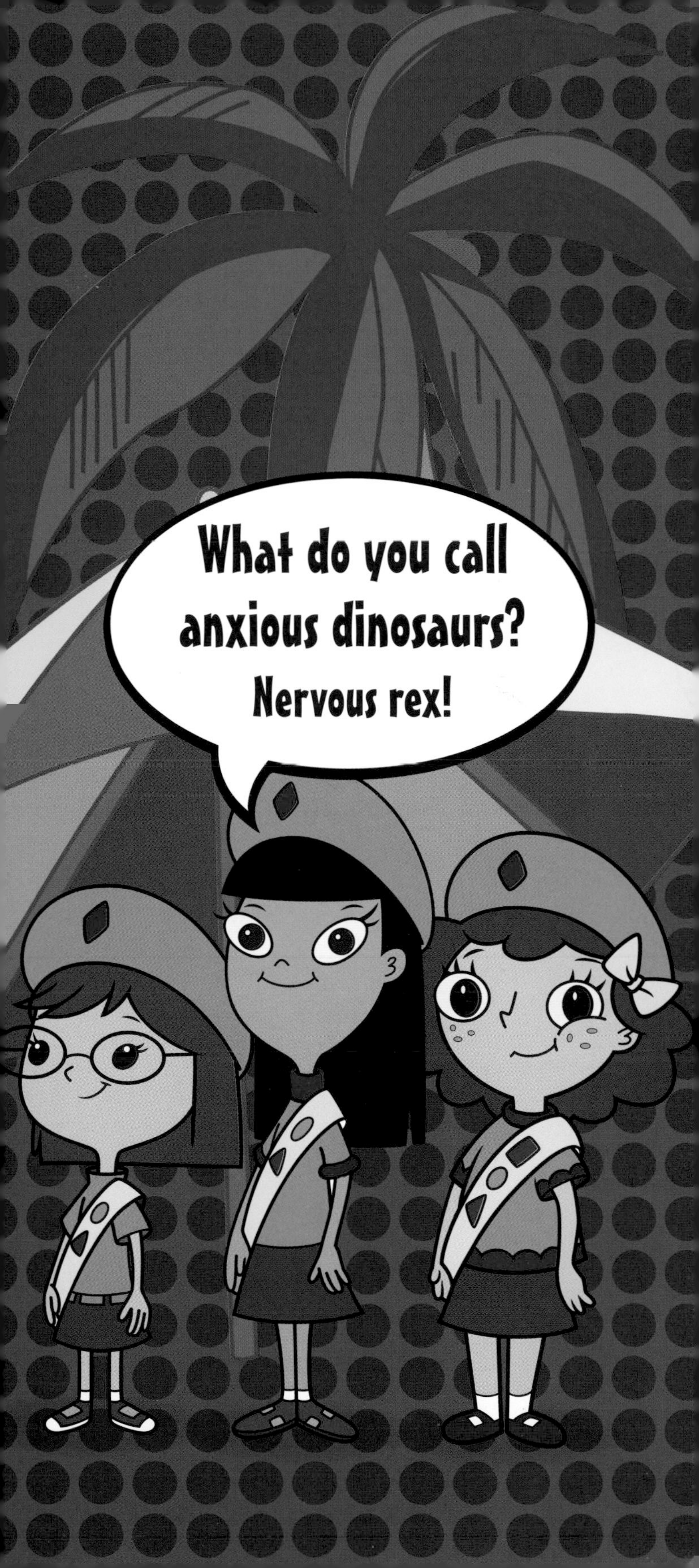
What do you call anxious dinosaurs?
Nervous rex!

What do you call a one-eyed dinosaur?

I-don't-think-he-saur-us!

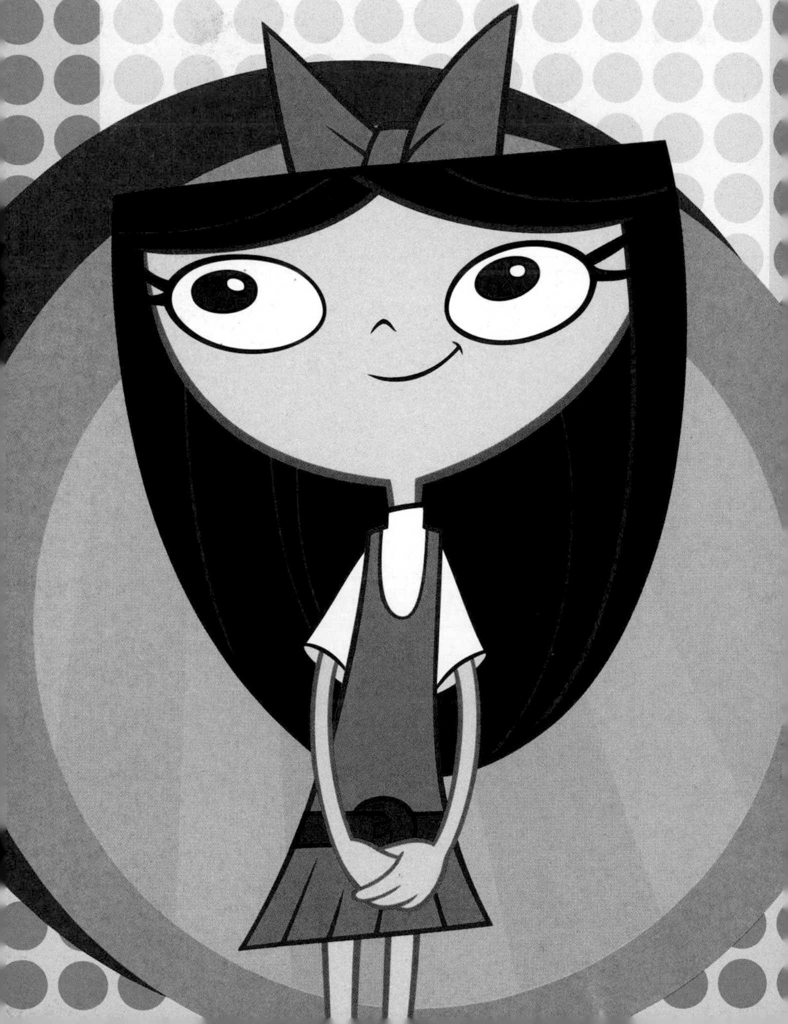

Why did the triceratops need a bandage?
He had a dino-sore!

Surf's Up!

Phineas and Ferb once built an entire beach – complete with sand, palm trees and waves for surfing – in the garden. Even Candace had an amazing time!

Why do fish swim in saltwater?

Because pepper makes them sneeze!

What do you call a shrimp with three eyes?

A shri*ii*imp!

Hey, we're almost done!

But here are a few more jokes before we go!

Why is six afraid of seven?

Because seven ate nine!

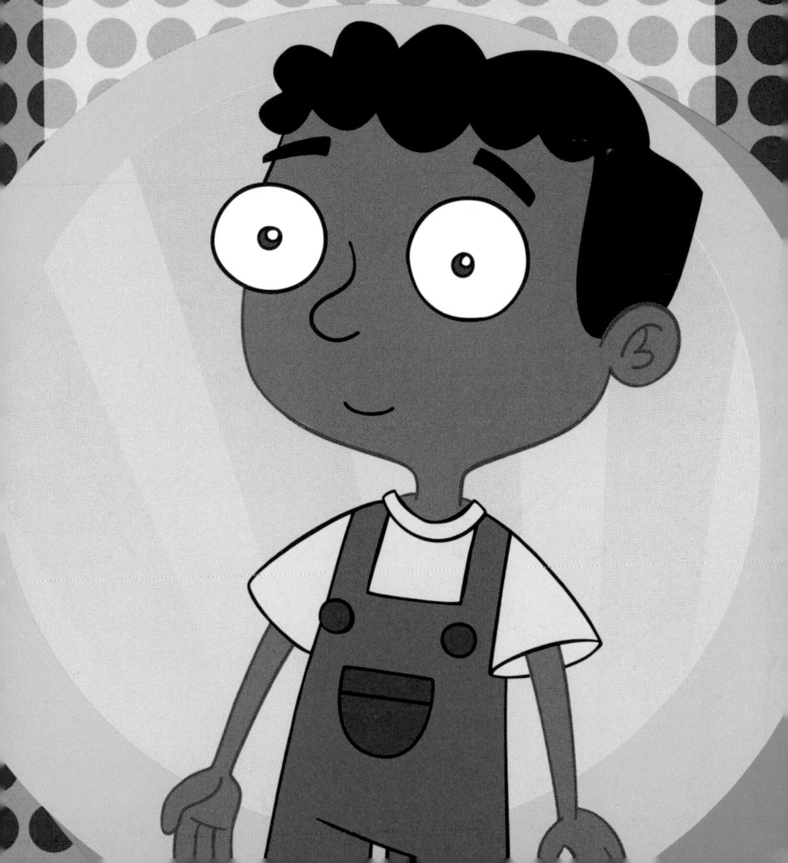

Why are fish so smart?
Because they live in schools!

What kind of cheese is made backwards?

Edam!

Why did the banana have to go to the doctor's office?

It didn't peel well!

Write your own jokes!

Think you're as funny as Phineas and Ferb? Well here's your chance to write your own jokes – then tell your friends and watch their sides split with laughter!

....

....

....

....

....

....

....

....

....

....

....

What are Phineas and Ferb saying to each other?

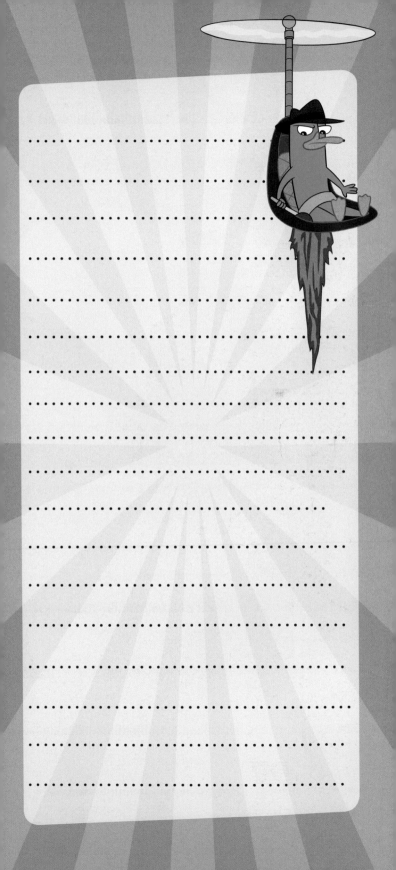

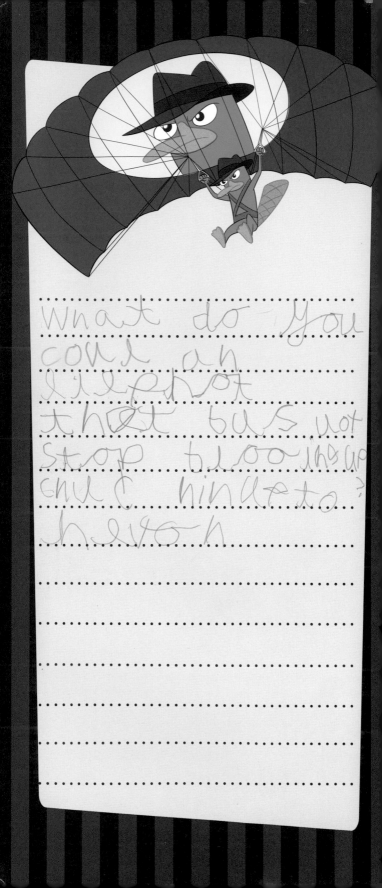

what do you
coul an
lilepilot
thet bus not
stop bloowingup
cnlc hindleto?
hlvon